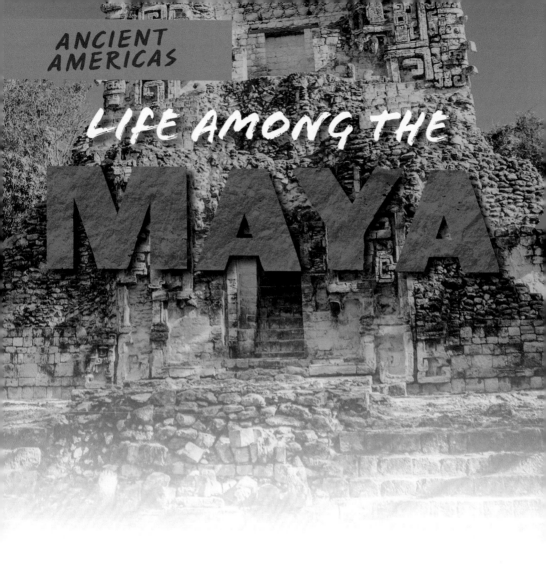

ANCIENT
AMERICAS

LIFE AMONG THE
MAYA

IAN MAHANEY

PowerKiDS
press.

NEW YORK

Published in 2017 by **The Rosen Publishing Group**
29 East 21st Street, New York, NY 10010

Developed and produced for Rosen by BlueAppleWorks Inc.

Editors for BlueAppleWorks Inc. : Melissa McClellan, Marcia Abramson
Designers: Haley Harasymiw, T.J. Choleva
Illustrator: Joshua Avramson

Picture credits: Cover: frgrd. prochasson frederic/Shutterstock; bkgrd. Gerald Marella/Shutterstock. Back
cover: frgrd. Artishok/Shutterstock; bkgrd. altanaka/Shutterstock. Title page Lev Levin/Shutterstock; p.
5 AlejandroLinaresGarcia/Creative Commons; p. 9 FA2010/Public Domain; p.10 Pedro Szekely/Creative
Commons; p. 13 Leon Rafael/Shutterstock; p. 13 inset Leon Rafael/Shutterstock; p. 14 Simon Dannhauer/
Shutterstock; p. 16 left Daderot/Creative Commons; p. 16 middle Wolfgang Sauber/Creative Commons;
p. 16 right, 22 left Daderot/Public Domain; p. 17 left MickyWiswedel/Shutterstock; p. 17 Bjørn Christian
Tørrissen/Creative Commons; p. 18 left Peter Hermes Furian/Shutterstock; p. 18 piotreknik/Shutterstock;
p. 18 right Vadim Petrakov/Shutterstock; p. 19 Michel wal/Creative Commons; p. 21 Wollertz/Shutterstock;
p. 22 Inakiherrasti/Creative Commons; p.25 left Michel wal/Creative Commons; p. 25 Wolfgang Sauber/
Creative Commons; p. 25 right John Hill/Creative Commons; p. 27 Emanuel Leutze/Public Domain; p. 29
Patryk Kosmider/Shutterstock; p. 29 right Patryk Kosmider/Shutterstock; Maps: © T.J. Choleva/Shutterstock:
IndianSummer

Cataloging-in-Publication Data

Names: Mahaney, Ian.
Title: Life among the Maya / Ian Mahaney.
Description: New York : PowerKids Press, 2017. | Series: Ancient Americas | Includes index.
Identifiers: ISBN 9781508149880 (pbk.) | ISBN 9781508149828 (library bound) | ISBN 9781508149705 (6 pack)
Subjects: LCSH: Mayas--Juvenile literature. | Indians of Central America--Juvenile literature.
Classification: LCC F1435. M34 2017| DDC 972.81'016--dc23

Manufactured in the United States of America
CPSIA Compliance Information: Batch #BS16PK: For Further Information contact Rosen Publishing, New York, New York at 1-800-237-9932

CONTENTS

CHAPTER I

ANCIENT MAYA

Most **anthropologists** agree that the ancestors of all Native Americans—from those living in Alaska and Canada to Native Americans in South America—left Asia and walked to the Americas. During the last ice age that began between 120,000 and 60,000 years ago, sea levels dropped and exposed the sea floor of the narrow Bering Strait. This ice age lasted until 10,000 years ago. Historians think **nomadic** people from Siberia crossed the land bridge to Alaska at this time. They probably followed herds of animals they hunted east into Alaska. Some of these peoples settled in Alaska. Others moved east across Canada. Still others moved south and settled in the present-day continental United States. Additional people populated present-day Mexico and even further south into Central America then South America.

The Maya are descendants of peoples who moved to Mexico and Central America. Their civilization is between 3,000 and 4,000 years old.

Some historians think that the Mayan people descended from the Olmec people. The Olmec developed their culture around 1200 B.C. and lived for about 800 years in southern Mexico. They built pyramids and developed a writing system. The giant stone heads that they carved still stand today.

THE GIANT HEADS CARVED BY
THE OLMECS LIKELY DEPICT
ANCIENT GODS AND RULERS.

Some are more than 10 feet (3 m) tall and weigh more than 20 tons (18 metric tons). Yet the Olmecs vanished, possibly because of changes in their environment.

Historians know that the two cultures have elements in common, but disagree on how much the Olmec influenced the Maya. Both are Mesoamerican cultures. "Meso" means middle, so "Mesoamerica" refers to the area from mid-Mexico to the northern part of Costa Rica, where advanced cultures developed before the arrival of Europeans.

The Maya first arrived in areas of southern Mexico and Central America between 1000 B.C. and 2000 B.C. The peak of their civilization lasted about 600 years, roughly between the years 250 A.D. until 900 A.D. They lived in and around the Yucatán Peninsula of what is now Mexico.

Unlike the Aztecs and Incas, the Mayan people did not live in a single empire or kingdom. Instead the Maya lived in multiple kingdoms or a collection of communities called city-states. Each community was a city surrounded by land for farming. Kings in each city-state ruled the land and population.

What's in the name?

The people we call Maya did not use that name for themselves until later in their history. Spanish explorers may have derived the name from Mayapan, an ancient city.

Mayan civilization collapsed after its peak. **Archaeologists** and anthropologists still can't explain the cause of the collapse. Some think drought caused the collapse. Others think war, disease, excess farming, famine, overpopulation, or climate change may have affected Mayan civilization.

The remaining Maya, living in smaller communities, first met Spanish explorers in 1502. Beginning in the sixteenth century, the Spanish **conquistadors** invaded and colonized lands in modern day Mexico and Central America. The Spanish eventually conquered the Maya, like all other Mesoamerican peoples. The Spanish reorganized Mayan states into areas that the Spanish could control better.

North America

Atlantic Ocean

Gulf of Mexico

Mesoamerica

Tikal

Uxmal

Yucatán Peninsula

North America

South America

South America

Central America

Pacific Ocean

CHAPTER 2

MAYAN CIVILIZATION

Mayan civilization is usually sorted into three eras, the Preclassic, Classic, and Postclassic periods. The Preclassic era spans 1,300 to 2,300 years beginning at the time the Maya first lived in Mexico and Central America. During the Preclassic era, the Maya settled on the coasts in modern day Mexico and other Central American countries. They moved inland afterwards. The Maya began growing corn during this time period.

Mayan civilization peaked during the Classic period. Beginning around 250 A.D. through 900 A.D., the Maya developed a sophisticated culture. They wrote with **hieroglyphs**. They built pyramids and constructed massive stone buildings. The Maya studied astronomy and math, and created complex calendars.

Mayan civilization collapsed after the Classic period. The Maya left cities. They abandoned pyramids and temples. The Maya didn't disappear, though. Instead, the culture concentrated in the Yucatán Peninsula in Mexico. In fact, Mayan culture continued into the Postclassic period. The Postclassic Mayan period ended when the Maya met Spanish conquistadors.

DETAILED CARVINGS CHRONICLE
MAYAN HISTORY AND CULTURE
ON BUILDINGS AND MONUMENTS.

MAYAN CITY-STATES

During the peak period of Mayan civilization there were about 60 city-states each with approximately 60,000 people. Mayan city-states frequently traded with one another. Sometimes the city-states formed **alliances** to protect themselves. They often needed protection because city-states also fought with each other. In fact, the Maya fought a lot.

The ajaw was the ruler or king of a city-state. He sent noblemen and common people to fight wars. They fought to capture territory, but also resources such as water and land for agriculture. The people of Mayan city-states fought to capture live prisoners, too. An army that seized an opponent's noblemen might **sacrifice** these elites to Mayan gods. The victors might **decapitate** the ajaw and enslave the commoners.

TIKAL, IN NORTHERN GUATEMALA, WAS A MAJOR MAYA CITY. TODAY IT IS AN IMPORTANT ARCHAEOLOGICAL SITE.

The people of the Maya city-states believed their kings descended from their gods. Some kings took the name of a god, and royal blood was used in religious ceremonies.

LEADERSHIP, SOCIAL CLASSES

Mayan city-states housed several classes of people. The ajaw sat at the top. He passed his title, nobility, and ruling powers to his eldest son. The noblemen consisted of wealthy members of the city-state. They elected fellow nobles to ruling positions. Some nobles negotiated alliances with neighboring city-states. Others were military leaders and supervisors. The nobles also elected priests. Priests performed religious ceremonies and carried out human sacrifices. They cut the hearts out of victims before offering them to the gods. Mayan priests were also the intellectuals. They studied math and astronomy. They were responsible for the administration and organization of the city-state.

The bulk of Mayan people were commoners. Anthropologists think at least 90 percent of the Maya were common people. Most of them lived on the land that surrounded the city. They farmed. They built temples. Some also worked as artists and merchants. Though commoners could build wealth and live comfortably, they were not nobles. A commoner, no matter how wealthy, could never wear a nobleman's clothing. Commoners and nobles were separate classes of people.

CHAPTER 3

ARCHITECTURE AND SCIENCES

The Maya built great cities, palaces, and temples out of the local limestone and sandstone. Although they had no metal tools, no wheeled carts, and no beasts of burden to pull heavy loads, they were able to build cities that still stand today, centuries after the decline of their civilization.

Archaeologists consider Uxmal (shown at right) an excellent example of a typical Maya city. The cities did not all have the same layout, because they were built around the local geography, but they all had plazas, palaces, terraced pyramids, ball courts, sweat baths, and religious sites.

The Maya used a kind of cement or mud as **mortar** to hold stones together, then decorated the outside of their buildings with carvings and sculptures. Sometimes the outside was covered with a plaster-like material called stucco, and painted with bright colors. Inside walls likely were painted brightly too, with murals that depicted historical or religious scenes. Mica, a shiny mineral, was added to make paint sparkle for special occasions.

Important buildings, with elaborate decorations, usually were clustered near the center of Maya cities, while ordinary people lived outside the city center in simple huts made of hay and stucco.

MAYAN MURALS, LIKE THE ONE
AT RIGHT, LIKELY COVERED THE
INTERIOR WALLS AT UXMAL AND
OTHER GREAT CITIES.

PLAZAS AND PALACES

The Maya built at least one plaza at the center of city-states. They filled the plazas with ball courts, walkways, and trees. They surrounded the plazas with huge buildings such as pyramids and palaces. The Maya built huge structures. One of the biggest buildings the Maya constructed was a palace near a marketplace in the Mayan city of Cancuen. Set in modern day Guatemala, the palace had 170 rooms, 3 stories, and ceilings that are 66 feet (20 m) tall.

MAYAN PYRAMIDS

The Mayans are famous for their pyramids, which they used both for religious rites and burials of important people. Many of the pyramids were designed to hold religious ceremonies. These pyramids had steep stairs,

THE TEMPLE OF THE GREAT JAGUAR WAS BUILT OVER A KING'S TOMB IN TIKAL. ITS NAME COMES FROM ONE OF ITS CARVINGS.

TOWERS OF TIKAL

Tikal was the capital of an important city-state called Mutul in what is now northern Guatemala. As many as 90,000 people once lived there. To serve so many people, the Maya built five tall pyramids in the city center, each one more than 200 feet (60 m) tall, with temples on top. The tallest one honors an eighth century king. Many smaller pyramids also have been found, along with ruins of even more. Today Tikal is a national park and archaeological site where new discoveries are still being made.

but priests and other people still were able to climb them. A small temple was built on the flat top, where sacrifices were made to the gods.

If a temple was dedicated to a god, the stairs were built even steeper. No one was allowed to climb them or even touch them. Inside, some of these pyramids were designed with doors, tunnels, and traps that led nowhere. This was done to keep people from bothering the gods.

Kings or other powerful people were buried in small rooms inside some of the pyramids. Often they were buried with their treasures, such as jade jewelry and jaguar skins.

Historians believe the Mayan pyramids also served as landmarks, soaring up over the jungle to a height of as much as 230 feet (70 m) and helping people find their way. One seaside pyramid may have been built with windows on top so it would serve as a kind of lighthouse for Mayan sea traders.

RELIGION AND WORSHIP

The Maya designed and built some pyramids so they were difficult to climb. Only priests ascended their steps to perform rituals while close to the many Mayan gods. In total, the Maya worshiped at least 165 gods ranging from the water god who prevented drought to the sun god to the **maize** god.

The Maya also celebrated and worshiped nature. They paid close attention to the seasons, and the sun's and moon's positions in the skies. They celebrated seasonal change. They observed the **equinoxes** and **solstices** with festivals. The Maya included exact calculations for solstices and equinoxes in the design of their cities. Of the Mayan temples in Tikal, they built one temple so that it lies exactly west of a second temple at both equinoxes.

THE MAYA CREATED MANY CLAY SCULPTURES OF RELIGIOUS FIGURES. FROM LEFT TO RIGHT ARE A FERTILITY AND LIGHTNING GOD, A PRIEST, AND A FIRE GOD.

MATH AND CALENDARS

To help them practice their religion, the Mayas became excellent astronomers and mathematicians. Historians believe the Maya and other Mesoamerican civilizations were far ahead of the rest of the world in developing accurate calendars.

The Maya were among the first people in the world to understand that zero was a number. The Maya built a number system based on groups of 20. We use base 10. They wrote numbers vertically while we write numbers horizontally. They based their calendars on this number system.

The Maya used a three-part calendar that was very complex to determine the day, month, and year.

17

The tzolk'in was a religious calendar with 260 days divided into 20 periods. The haab was a solar calendar with 365 days divided into 18 months of 20 days and one final short month of 5 days. A third calendar, known as the long count, determined the year.

A date was established by finding the intersection of the tzolk'in and the haab. To do this, the Maya created calendar wheels in which the two calendars interlock. At the end of 52 years, the tzolk'in and haab start their new year, and a new cycle, on the same day.

Some Maya peoples still use the calendar wheel today.

THE MESOAMERICAN WHEEL CALENDAR, REVOLVING AROUND THE FACE OF THE SUN GOD, DATES BACK AT LEAST 2,500 YEARS.

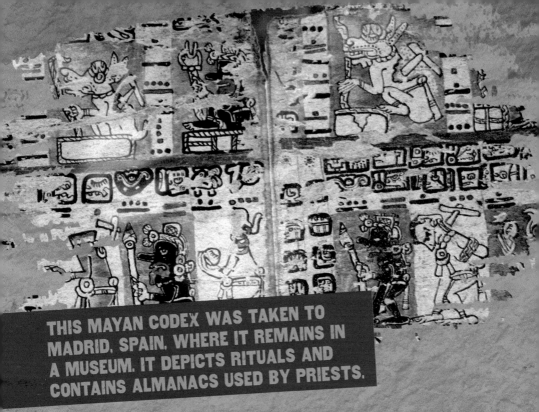

MAYAN WRITING SYSTEM

Beginning in the Preclassic period, the Maya developed the most advanced writing system of all the pre-Columbian Native Americans. It was a system of more than 800 symbols mainly based on hieroglyphs, but also on **phonetics**. The Maya told stories in their pictures and recorded these stories on stone, ceramics, and stelae. Stelae were slabs of stone often found surrounding the great plazas of Mayan cities. The Maya also recorded stories in sculptures and in a type of book called a codex. Codices are also called screen fold books because they are made from long sheets of paper then folded like screens or fans into a book. Few codices exist today, as most were burned by Spanish conquerors trying to eliminate the native Maya culture.

CHAPTER 4

LIFE IN MAYAN SOCIETY

The Maya lived in a tropical region with thick forests, few rivers and lakes, and poor soil for farming. They had to adapt to both wet and dry seasons in order to grow food and build their civilization. They prayed to nature-based gods to help them live in their rainforest environment.

FARMING METHODS

The Maya developed a system of agriculture in the rainforest. Normally, water flooded the soil and therefore any crops the Maya planted. To compensate, the Maya built elaborate canals to divert water from the fields. The Maya used soil they dug from the canals to raise their planting beds above the **water table**.

The Maya suffered long dry seasons in Mexico and Central America. They prepared by storing water during the rainy season. In Tikal, the Maya built dams and reservoirs to collect water. They moved water to their fields with canals during drier times.

Precious cacao beans

Mesoamericans loved chocolate, which they made from cacao beans. The beans were so valuable that they were used as currency.

TODAY THE JUNGLE HAS
CREPT BACK OVER MANY
MAYAN RUINS.

The Maya farmed with simple tools made of stone and wood. They used an ancient farming method called slash and burn. The farmers burned old crops on a plot of land then planted new crops and used the ashes for fertilizer.

Corn, or maize, was the most important crop. The Maya considered corn sacred and worshiped a corn god. They made corn into tortillas, a drink called atole, and even a kind of beer. They found many uses for the husks.

The Maya also grew squash, sweet potatoes, tomatoes, beans, and chili peppers. They cultivated fruits including papaya, banana, avocado, and guava, as well as their precious cacao.

MAYA FARMERS WOULD ASK BOTH THE RAIN GOD (LEFT) AND THE MAIZE GOD FOR GOOD HARVESTS.

TRAVELING TRADERS

Maya trading started with the neighborhood marketplace and reached out all the way into northern Mexico and throughout the Caribbean. The traders used dugout canoes that could carry as many as 25 paddlers. There was also a well-traveled land route.

The traders would exchange feathers, **obsidian**, gold, jade, pottery, honey, amber, animal pelts, cotton fabric, incense, medicinal herbs, vegetable dyes, chili peppers, tools, toys, and bags of salt produced from sea water.

Merchants became an important and honored class in the city-states, and artisans were respected for their skill in creating ceramics and jewelry. Some historians believe that the king and the nobles controlled trade and profited the most from it, but others think there was more of a free market system.

MAYAN FAMILY STRUCTURE

Like many traditional families, Mayan families split duties between men and women. Men fought battles, hunted, and farmed. Their wives cared for the household and children, sewed clothing, weaved baskets, and cooked.

Families lived in stone or wood houses with thatched roofs made of corn. Their floors were mud. Families often lived with relatives. They did this so men could farm together. They brought harvests to their wives. The women ground corn into meal and made tortillas.

Children played an important role in Maya families. By the time they were five or six, boys were farming with their fathers and girls were working in the home with their mothers. By age 15, they were considered adults.

MAYAN ARTS AND CULTURE

The Maya were artists. They created much of their art to **complement** their spiritual world. For example, they sculpted burial masks made of jade for their ajaws. They also made sculptures for personal uses and to fill the central plazas. The Maya drew. They made clay pots. They often added hieroglyphs to their ceramics and sculptures to tell stories. The Maya wrote poetry and they passed stories of their people from generation to generation. They played music and danced in beautiful and elaborate costumes.

MAYAN BALL GAMES

The Maya set up ball courts in the cities to play a game called pitz, pok a tok, and other names. The game was played with a rubber ball about 20 inches (51 cm) in diameter on a stone court. The walls of the court slanted inward. Stone rings were hung high up on the walls, and players tried to shoot the ball through the rings, like basketball. The game was also like soccer, as players were not allowed to use their hands. The game often ended when someone did manage to score.

Precious jade

Jade, a hard green rock, was a symbol of good to the Maya, who valued it more than gold. They cut and polished jade into jewelry, tools, and ritual objects.

THIS EXPRESSIVE FUNERAL MASK WAS CARVED OUT OF JADE FOR PAKAL, A KING OF PALENQUE IN THE SEVENTH CENTURY.

According to Mayan stories, gods of the heavens played the first game of pitz versus the rulers of the underworld. In this way, the ball court was seen as a portal to the Mayan underworld. This gave the games a religious component. While the winners became heroes, the captain or even the whole losing team could be sacrificed to the gods. Sometimes two feuding city-states would choose to settle their differences with the game instead of going to war.

In other ways the games were much like sports today. High-ranking nobles, priests, and everyday people came to watch. Sacred music was played and people gambled on which side would win!

CHAPTER 5

DOWNFALL AND LEGACY

Famed explorer Christopher Columbus, born in Italy and sailing for Spain, encountered the Maya in the Gulf of Mexico in 1502. It likely was the first time the Maya had met Europeans. After Columbus died in Spain in 1506, other Spanish explorers sailed near Mayan lands.

The explorers exposed the Maya to smallpox and other diseases. The Maya had never seen these diseases and many died. Of the 7 million Maya at the time, scientists estimate 90 percent died of these new diseases.

In 1519, the Spanish began their conquest of Mexico and areas of Central America. The Spanish wanted to defeat the Maya, Aztecs, and all other Native Americans in Mexico. The Spanish sought wealth and they wanted to establish a colony. By 1524, the Spanish had invaded and defeated Mayan city-states. The Spanish established their own capitals and set up their own rulers. In 1527, the Spanish invaded the Mayan population in the Yucatán Peninsula. The Spanish failed. They tried again and failed. It took 19 years amid Mayan resistance for the Spanish to conquer the Yucatán. At the same time, the Maya revolted in areas the Spanish controlled. It took the Spanish another 151 years, until 1697, to subdue the Maya and control all the Mayan territories.

THE AZTECS FELL QUICKLY TO ARMORED
SPANISH INVADERS LED BY HERNÁN CORTÉS
(SHOWN IN ILLUSTRATION) BUT THE MAYA
FOUGHT FOR 170 YEARS.

27

THE COLUMBUS CONNECTION

The Maya first met Europeans in 1502 when Christopher Columbus sent his brother Bartholomew in a ship to check out some islands near Honduras. His thirteen-year-old son Fernando was aboard, too. The Spaniards were surprised when a large Mayan trading canoe appeared, filled with well-dressed traders and some of their families. They carried an impressive array of goods, including beautiful clothing, obsidian knives, ceramics, copper goods, tortillas, and corn beer, which young Fernando reported enjoying. The Spaniards took the ship's captain to serve as an interpreter, but let the others go peacefully. Soon they sent the captain home, too, with gifts for his service. Columbus went off in a different direction and so did not discover the Maya city-states.

By contrast, the Spanish invaded the Aztec empire in 1519 and defeated them by 1521. In 1532, the Spanish defeated the Incas. The Spanish quieted Inca resistance by 1572. The Spanish included all these areas into their colony New Spain.

The Spanish banned Mayan religion. They tried to convert the Mayan people to Christianity. The Spanish were successful in converting some Maya. Other Mayan people lived in such remote areas that the **missionaries** had trouble finding them. The Spanish enslaved many Mayan people. The Spanish also destroyed most Mayan books. Few books with hieroglyphs survive to this day.

Mayan culture survives, though. The Maya still live in areas of Mexico, Guatemala, Belize, El Salvador, and Honduras.

There are between 7 and 8 million Maya today. Some Maya even live in the United States. Many of these Mayan people hold onto their culture. They live in an ancient Mayan yet a modern world. Women still cook traditional foods such as tamales and tortillas. They make traditional clothing and weave beautiful baskets. Men farm their land using traditional tools. Children study Spanish and Mayan languages. The Maya still speak more than 20 Mayan languages today. One of most important Mayan languages is Yucatec. The Maya speak it in the Yucatán Peninsula.

Tourists worldwide have an interest in Mayan culture and tradition. Tourists can visit and climb ancient Mayan pyramids. They can see the rainforests. Modern Maya even sell crafts such as sculptures and calendars. Some Maya are insistent. They are keeping their culture in a modern world.

CULTURAL REENACTMENTS HELP TODAY'S MAYA PRESERVE AND SHARE THEIR HERITAGE.

GLOSSARY

alliances: groups of countries, states, or people working together toward a common goal

anthropologists: scientists who study the history and society of humans

archaeologists: scientists who study the remains of peoples from the past to understand how they lived

complement: to make something better or more complete

conquistadors: the explorers and soldiers sent by Spain to conquer the New World

decapitate: to cut someone's head off

equinox: the two days of the year when night and day are the same length. Equinoxes fall on or near March 20 and September 22.

hieroglyphs: pictures that form a system of writing

maize: corn

missionaries: people who go to a foreign country to do religious work

mortar: a wet substance put between bricks or stones that holds them together after it hardens

nomadic: roaming about from place to place

obsidian: a shiny, black volcanic glass used to make tools and jewelry

phonetics: the sounds of speech

sacrifice: to make a gift of another's body to the gods

solstice: the two days of the year when the sun appears farthest north or south of the equator. The solstices fall on or near June 22 and December 22.

water table: the boundary in soil where the soil is saturated with water below and relatively dry above

FOR MORE INFORMATION

BOOKS

Hibbert, Clare. *The History Detective Investigates: Mayan Civilization*. New York: Hachette Children's Group, 2014.

Lechner, Judith. *The Maya*. New Rochelle, NY: Benchmark Education, 2011.

Schuman, Michael. *Maya and Aztec Mythology Rocks!* New York: Enslow, 2011.

Tieck, Sarah. *Maya*. North Mankato, Minnesota: ABDO Publishing, 2015.

WEBSITES

Due to the changing nature of Internet links, PowerKids Press has developed an online list of websites related to the subject of this book. This site is updated regularly. Please use this link to access the list:

www.powerkidslinks.com/aa/maya

INDEX